THE LAW OF EVIDENCE
IN A NUTSHELL

Scholarly Articles by Peter Fritz Walter

The Law of Evidence

The Restriction of National Sovereignty

Alternative Medicine and Wellness Techniques

Consciousness and Shamanism

Creative Prayer

Soul Jazz

The Ego Matter

The Star Script

The Lunar Bull

Basics of Mythology

Basics of Feng Shui

Power or Depression?

The Mythology of Narcissism

Normative Psychoanalysis

Notes on Consciousness

Patterns of Perception

Sane Child vs. Insane Society

Basics of the Science of Mind

The Secret Science

Oedipal Hero

Processed Reality

THE LAW OF EVIDENCE IN A NUTSHELL

Basics for Law School

by Peter Fritz Walter

Published by Sirius-C Media Galaxy LLC

113 Barksdale Professional Center, Newark, Delaware, USA

©2015 Peter Fritz Walter. Some rights reserved.

2017 Revised, Updated and Reformatted Edition

Creative Commons Attribution 4.0 International License

This publication may be distributed, used for an adaptation or for derivative works, also for commercial purposes, as long as the rights of the author are attributed. The attribution must be given to the best of the user's ability with the information available. Third party licenses or copyright of quoted resources are untouched by this license and remain under their own license.

The moral right of the author has been asserted

Set in Palatino

Designed by Peter Fritz Walter

ISBN 978-1-515157-06-9

Publishing Categories
Law / Evidence

Publisher Contact Information
publisher@sirius-c-publishing.com
http://sirius-c-publishing.com

Author Contact Information
pfw@peterfritzwalter.com

About Dr. Peter Fritz Walter
http://peterfritzwalter.com

About the Author

Parallel to an international law career in Germany, Switzerland and the United States, Dr. Peter Fritz Walter (Pierre) focused upon fine art, cookery, astrology, musical performance, social sciences and humanities.

He started writing essays as an adolescent and received a high school award for creative writing and editorial work for the school magazine.

After finalizing his law diplomas, he graduated with an LL.M. in European Integration at Saarland University, Germany, in 1982, and with a Doctor of Law title from University of Geneva, Switzerland, in 1987.

He then took courses in psychology at the University of Geneva and interviewed a number of psychotherapists in Lausanne and Geneva, Switzerland. His interest was intensified through a hypnotherapy with an Ericksonian American hypnotherapist in Lausanne. This led him to the recovery and healing of his inner child.

After a second career as a corporate trainer and personal coach, Pierre retired in 2004 as a full-time writer, philosopher and consultant.

His nonfiction books emphasize a systemic, holistic, cross-cultural and interdisciplinary perspective, while his fiction works and short stories focus upon education, philosophy, perennial wisdom, and the poetic formulation of an integrative worldview.

Pierre is a German-French bilingual native speaker and writes English as his 4th language after German, Latin and French. He also reads source literature for his research works in Spanish, Italian, Portuguese, and Dutch. In addition, Pierre has notions of Thai, Khmer, Chinese, Japanese, and Vietnamese.

All of Pierre's books are hand-crafted and self-published, designed by the author. Pierre publishes via his Delaware company, Sirius-C Media Galaxy LLC, and under the imprints of IPUBLICA and SCM (Sirius-C Media).

It is not the law of evidence's business to say what [...] facts are in any particular case. They are determined by the substantive law or by the proceedings.'

—Phipson and Elliott, Manual of the Law of Evidence, 11th Edition, by D. W. Elliott, London: Sweet & Maxwell, 1980, 15.

The author's profits from this book are being donated to charity.

Contents

Chapter One — 9
What is Evidence?

Chapter Two — 11
What is a Fact?

Chapter Three — 13
The Burden of Proof

Introduction — 13
The Evidential Burden — 23
- Introduction — 23
- Notion and Function — 25
- Standard of Proof — 28
- Incidence — 33

The Persuasive Burden — 37
- Standard of Proof — 37
- Notion and Function — 44
- Incidence — 46

Bibliography — 53
Contextual Bibliography

Personal Notes — 63

Chapter One

What is Evidence?

This booklet for law students provides an outline of the general principles of the law of evidence.

What is evidence?

Here is a widely shared definition: 'All legal means, exclusive of mere argument, which tend to prove or disprove any matter of fact, the truth of which is submitted to judicial investigation.'

> —James Bradley Tayer, A Preliminary Treatise on Evidence, 1898.

Chapter Two

What is a Fact?

Only facts are subject to proof. Thus, the evidence procedure always relates to facts.

Now, what is a fact?

According to Wigmore, fact means 'whatever is the subject of perception and consciousness.'

> —John Henry Wigmore, Evidence in Trials at Common Law, A Treatise on the Anglo-American System of Evidence in Trials at Common Law, 10 Volumes, Vol. 9 'Evidence in Trials at Common Law', rev. by James H. Chadburn, Boston: Toronto: Little, Brown & Co., 1981, §§1, 2.

Facts subject to proof are those that are 'facts in issue' and 'facts relevant to the issue,' or else 'facts probative to an issue.' (Id.)

The main facts in issue are those that the plaintiff must prove in a civil action if he is to win, and those that the defendant must prove in order to establish a defense.

It is either substantive law or adjective law, i.e. procedural law, which determines those facts.

In the words of Phipson and Elliott: 'It is not the law of evidence's business to say what those facts are in any particular case. They are determined by the substantive law or by the proceedings.'

> —Phipson and Elliott, Manual of the Law of Evidence, 11th Edition, by D. W. Elliott, London: Sweet & Maxwell, 1980, 15.

Chapter Three

The Burden of Proof

Introduction

The rules governing the burden of demonstrating a fact to be true by evidence are intimately related to the rules governing the burden of alleging a fact.

As a general rule, the party who has the burden of pleading also has the burden of proof.

The affirmative burden is applied to the pleadings and establishes a certain order in the probatory procedure; according to that order, the burden shifts from one party to the other.

However, the objective burden of proof is not related to the production of evidence, but decides the litigation in case of a *non liquet*, that is, an irresolvable doubt regarding any fact in question: the party who carries the objective burden, then, loses the case. This means, practically speaking, that the objective or *legal burden* enables the judge to render a verdict in a case where the truth cannot be found. It's the applicable substantive law that attributes the objective burden. It's also correct to denote this burden as the *ultimate burden*, as it does not shift.

> ### James & Hazard
> A leading characteristic of the Anglo-American procedural system is its adversary nature. In civil disputes it is generally up to the parties, not the court, to initiate and prosecute litigation, to investigate the pertinent facts, and to present proof and legal argument to the tribunal. The court's function, in general, is limited to adjudicating the issues submitted to it by the parties on the proof presented by them, and to applying appropriate

> procedural sanctions upon motion of a party.
>
> —James, Fleming James & Geoffrey Hazard, Geoffrey, Civil Procedure, 2nd Edition, Toronto: Little, Brown & Company, 1977, §1.2, 4 [45]

In fact, because of the particular nature of the adversary litigation system and its bestowal of judicial cognition upon both judge and jury, evidence law in general, and the rules of the burden of proof, in particular, have a much higher importance under common law than in continental law.

It is to note that statutory regulations on civil procedure seldom contain rules of evidence or a precise allocation of the burden of proof, as for example the UK's Civil Evidence Acts of 1968 and 1972, or South Africa's Civil Proceedings Evidence Act No. 25 of 1965.

This is systemically sound because the burden of proof is determined by the applicable substantive law, not civil procedure regulations.

There are however presumptions to be found in American civil procedure laws, in the rules No. 301 of the Federal Rules of Evidence (28 U.S.C.A.) and in the Uniform Rules of Evidence, 13 U.L.A. Civ. Proc. 227. A detailed regulation of evidence rules was worked out by the *American Law Institute* and was inserted in the *Model Code of Evidence (1942)*.

Similar rules are to be found in the California Evidence Code. As to Canada, the *Uniform Evidence Act* contains very detailed provisions regarding the burden of proof.

The general rule is that the judge adjudicates about legal questions, while the jury decides about the facts, but there are several exceptions to this rule.

In addition, it has to be seen that more and more litigations are held without a jury; in these cases, the judge is said to take over the two functions in one person. However, in principle, the particularities and rules of the burden of proof have not changed for that reason. Phipson & Elliott write: 'Now the trial is usually before the judge alone, but the two separate functions remain. The judge performs them both, but he must take care to keep them separate.'

> —Phipson & Elliott, Manual of the Law of Evidence (1980), 37

It is important to remember that evidence law has been marked by the particularity of the jury trial, and that is why the strict separation of the functions of judge and jury even applies when the judge decides alone.

In the United States, the *Federal Rules of Evidence* detail the evidence procedure in federal jurisdiction. These rules, interestingly, also do not make a distinction between trials with or without jury, as they implicitly hold that for the latter category of trials, the judge performs both functions.

> —Sir Rupert Cross, Cross on Evidence, 5th edition., London: Butterworths, 1979, 92 and Graham C. Lilly, Introduction to the Law of Evidence, St. Paul (West), 1978, 47, note 13

The main difficulty in understanding the concept of the burden of proof results from the fact that the term has more than one meaning.

It was only at the end of the 19th century that, with the classical monograph of J. B.

Tayer, *A Preliminary Treatise on Evidence (1898)*, the legal profession began to build awareness about the need to clarify the matter. James & Hazard note:

> ### JAMES & HAZARD
>
> The term burden of proof is used in our law to refer to two separate and quite different concepts. The distinction was not clearly perceived until it was pointed out by James Bradley Thayer in 1898. The decisions before that time and many later ones are hopelessly confused in reasoning about the problem. The two different concepts may be referred to as
> (1) the risk of non-persuasion, or the burden of persuasion or simply persuasion burden;
> (2) the duty of producing evidence, or simply the production burden or the burden of evidence.
>
> —James & Hazard, Civil Procedure (1977), §7.5, 240-241

The two burdens have to be distinguished; they are called *principle burdens*.

So far there is unanimity in the literature; on the details, however, the literature greatly vacillates. Cross distinguishes further between provisional and ultimate burden and between shifting burdens and rebuttable presumptions. Sometimes even a third burden is added, that is called the burden of pleadings, while in reality this burden is a consequence of the legal burden.

> —Graham, Federal Rules of Evidence in a Nutshell, St. Paul (Minn.): American Textbook Series, 1981, §301.3, 42

And Phipson to add a 4th burden, the burden of establishing the admissibility of the evidence.

> —Phipson on Evidence, 13th ed., by John Huxley Buzzard, Richard May and M. N. Howard, London: Sweet & Maxwell, 1982, 44, n. 4-03

THE BURDEN OF PROOF

In fact, the admissibility of proof by the judge is of high importance in the adversary trial as lay persons are going to decide about the evidence; as a result, it is crucial which evidence is admitted and which is refused by the judge, whose role is to supervise the trial game with his 'legal eye,' as juries can be rather unpredictable in their verdicts.

But apart from this rather fancy expansion of the system, most authors and the overwhelming number of precedents admit a dualistic system with two principle burdens.

> —See, for example, Gerard, Nash, Civil Procedure, Cases and Text, Sydney: The Law Book Company Ltd., 1976, 32, Paul F. Rothstein, State and Federal Rules, 2nd edition, St. Paul (West), 1981, Ch. II, 99

These principle burdens are:

(1) The *persuasive burden, legal burden* or *risk of non-persuasion of the jury;*

(2) The *evidential burden, burden of adducing evidence* or *duty of producing evidence to the judge.*

The presentation of evidence is a regulated and orderly ritual. It starts with the party who bears the evidential burden to address their proof to the judge.

The judge decides if a *prima facie case* has been made, and then instructs the jury to pronounce the final decision regarding the evidence offered by both parties.

This is often expressed in the terms that the parties have to 'pass the judge and convince the jury'.

> —See, for example, Phipson and Elliott (1980), 52

It's in that moment that the *persuasion burden* comes to play its decisive role.

—The formulation used in two U.S. district court decisions shows the nature of both burdens very well: 'Burden of proof has two elements, the burden of producing evidence and the burden of persuading the fact finder,' Abilene Sheet Metal Inc. v. N.L.R.B., 619 F.2d 332 (3d Cir. 1980) and Hochgurtel v. San Felippo, 253 N.W.2d 526, 78 Wis.2d 70 (Wis. 1977)

THE EVIDENTIAL BURDEN

INTRODUCTION

There is a special relationship between the expressions *evidential burden, prima facie evidence* and *standard of proof.*

The party that bears the persuasive burden has the right to begin with presenting evidence to the judge, and as a general rule, the evidential burden follows the persuasive or legal burden.

> —See Cross on Evidence (1979), 29, Phipson & Elliott (1980), 63

If, exceptionally, the legal burden is on the defendant, it's the defendant who has the right to begin. The right to begin also has been called 'onus probandi.'

As in principle the legal burden is on the plaintiff, it's the plaintiff who usually begins to produce evidence. For every single issue, evidence is thus produced.

This is not a particularity of civil procedure, but a general principle. We already learnt that every proof must relate to a specific fact in issue, otherwise it would be off-track and irrelevant.

As a result, a burden of proof 'in general' is inconceivable. For every fact in issue, there is a burden of proof that one of the parties is charged with.

Cross on Evidence expresses it this way: 'In the context of the law of evidence, the expression 'burden of proof' is meaningless unless it is used with reference to a particular issue.' (Id., 29).

The judge considers the evidence in the light of the applicable *standard of proof* and decides if a *prima facie case* was established.

Standard of proof is a measure for the *adequateness* of the proof presented. All evidence must meet a certain standard to be adequate, to be sufficient; as a result, all evidence has to be evaluated by the judge for meeting the standard of proof applicable in the particular litigation.

Notion and Function

Cross on Evidence writes that the concept of the evidential burden is the product of trial by jury and the possibility of withdrawing an issue from that body. (Id., 87, 91). See also the *California Evidence Code (1965)* which stipulates:

> CALIFORNIA EVIDENCE CODE (1965)
> §110. 'Burden of producing evidence' means the obligation of a party to introduce evidence sufficient to avoid a ruling against him on the issue.

The Model *Code on Evidence (1942)* explains:

> RULE 1. ...
> (2) 'Burden of producing evidence of a fact' means the burden which is discharged when sufficient evidence is introduced to support a finding that the fact exists.
>
> —American Law Institute, Model Code on Evidence, Chestnut, Philadelphia, 1942

In fact, the notion is unknown in continental law systems, and for good reason. It only makes sense in the adversary trial system and when a jury decides about the facts; the judge's function is in so far one of controlling and instructing the lay persons composing the jury.

The burden of producing evidence is not an obligation or a duty; it simply represents a *risk*: the risk to not being able to produce evidence satisfactory to the court.

The judge considers the evidence submitted by the parties and decides if

- (i) the evidence has met the standard of proof; or
- (ii) the evidence has not met the standard of proof.

The judge considers *all evidence*, not only the one submitted by the party that bears the evidential burden. This means that the party who bears the onus of proof can profit from proof submitted by the adversary. Cross and Wilkins write:

Cross & Wilkins

> Although we speak of one party 'bearing' the burden of proof, or the burden of adducing evidence, it must be remembered that he may be able to rely on those parts of his adversary's evidence which are favorable for him.

—Sir Rupert Cross & Nancy Wilkins, An Outline of the Law of Evidence, 5th edition, London: Butterworths, 1980, 27. See also Model Code on Evidence (1942), p. 74: 'Neither the rules nor the decisions require that the evidence discharging either burden shall have been introduced by the party having the burden.'

Standard of Proof

When a *prima facie case* was made by the party who bears the evidential burden, and the judge decides that the evidence meets the applicable standard of proof, this has basically three consequences:

- (i) the burden of proof is discharged;
- (ii) the burden shifts to the other party;

- (iii) the fact is proven if the other party cannot discharge their burden.

 —Cross on Evidence (1979), 119-120 remarks that 'no precise formulae have been laid down with regard to the standard of proof required for the discharge of the evidential burden and, as this is not a matter upon which it can ever be necessary for a judge to direct a jury, there is no reason why it should ever become a subject of formulae'

The standard of proof regarding the evidential burden is not a matter that the judge must instruct the jury about; only the persuasive burden is.

This is so simply because the judge alone renders this decision.

Cross and Wilkins explain about the standard of proof for prima facie evidence that it necessitates *a finding that the fact is proved if the evidence is uncontradicted.*

> —Cross & Wilkins, An Outline of the Law of Evidence (1980), 20. See also Graham, Federal Rules of Evidence in a Nutshell (1981), §301.4, 43, and Phipson and Elliott, Manual of the Law of Evidence (1980), 60: '… if the evidence is believed, any reasonable man could infer that the fact exists.'

It flows from the principle of *fair trial* that each party must have the possibility to contradict the evidence submitted by the other party.

Consequently, when one party discharges their evidential burden, the other party gets the burden.

This can be imagined as one party 'inheriting' the burden form the other party, or that the burden is 'passed' from one party to the other within the litigation game.

> —Phipson and Elliott, Manual of the Law of Evidence (1980), 62: 'It has been seen that the discharge of the evidential burden by one side

> puts the other side under a similar burden, or, as it is often put, 'passes' the burden upon him'

This also has been called the *shifting* of the evidential burden, while it has to be seen that the persuasion burden never shifts.

The 'shifting' is of course a juridical metaphor; the pretended 'movement' of the burden is in reality the idea of an equitable partition of the trial risk. Eggleston writes:

Eggleston

> It is often said that although the legal burden of proof remains throughout the trial where it was at the beginning, the evidential burden may shift from one party to the other. All this really means is that as a case proceeds, one party or the other will produce evidence that, if it remained unchallenged, would entitle the party producing it to a decision in his favour. In this sense he can be said to have shifted the burden of proof to the other party.

— Sir Richard Eggleston, Evidence, Proof and Probability, 2nd edition, London: Weidenfels & Nicholson, 1983, 27

Another result that flows out from this system is that when a prima facie case was not refuted or 'rebutted,' the fact is considered to have been proven.

The court has no obligation to arrive at this conclusion, but there is a high probability that the court decides on the lines of an uncontradicted *prima face case*.

The only case a judge is obliged to render a verdict in a particular way is when a statute puts up a general rule that contains a *legal presumption*.

In case the presumption was not rebutted, the judge's verdict must follow the general rule stipulated in the statute.

Similarly, when the prima facie evidence was not meeting the applicable standard of proof, the judge must render a decision adverse to the burdened party.

> —Cross on Evidence (1979), 27, Graham, Federal Rules of Evidence in a Nutshell (1981), §301.4, 43

In this case, one could also speak of the risk of producing evidence satisfactory to the court was realized against the party who was charged with it.

Incidence

At the beginning of the trial, the evidential burden is with the party who bears the persuasive burden.

> —550(b) of the California Evidence Code stipulates: 'The burden of producing evidence as to a particular fact is initially on the party with

the burden of proof as to this fact'. (West's Ann.Cal.Evid.Code §550, Vol. 29B, 508).

As *Cross on Evidence* puts it: 'As a general rule, the burden of adducing evidence is borne by the party who bears the burden of proof.'

> —Cross on Evidence (1979), 95. See also Cross & Wilkins, An Outline of the Law of Evidence (1980), 29

When the evidential burden is discharged, it is said to shift to the other party.

Because of this assumed shifting of the evidential burden, and because it is temporarily with one and then the other party, it is also called provisional burden.

Lord Denning explains in *Brown v. Rolls Royce Ltd.*, [1960] 1 W.L.R. 210, 215 (H.L.):

> My Lords, the difference between the judges of the Court of Session turned to the onus of proof. (...) The difference of

opinion shows how important it is to distinguish between a 'legal burden,' properly so called, which is imposed by the law itself, and a 'provisional' burden which is raised by the state of the evidence.

As only at the onset of the trial the two burdens are united, at any other point in time during the trial a test has to be effected for the determination of who bears the evidential burden.

This test has been inserted in various statutes; here is the one provided by the *California Evidence Code*:

> CALIFORNIA EVIDENCE CODE
> §550 Party who has the burden of producing evidence
> (a) The burden of producing evidence as to a particular fact is on the party against whom a finding on that fact would be required in the absence of further evidence.
>
> —West's Ann.Cal.Evid.Code §550, Vol. 29B, p. 508

It is noteworthy in this context that also Nigeria's Evidence Act details in §136:

> §136 EVIDENCE ACT OF NIGERIA
> (1) In civil cases the burden of first proving the existence or nonexistence of a fact lies on the party against whom the judgment of the court would be given if no evidence were produced on either side, (…)
> (2) If such party adduces evidence which ought reasonably to satisfy a jury that the fact sought to be proved is established, the burden lies on the party against whom judgment would be given if no more evidence were adduced; and so on successively, until all the issues in the pleadings have been dealt with.
>
> —Reproduced in Akinola Aguda, Law and Practice Relating to Evidence in Nigeria, London: Sweet & Maxwell, 1980, n. 21-03.

The Persuasive Burden

Standard of Proof

We have already seen that the term *burden of proof*, in the sense to encompass both evidential and persuasive burden, and the term *standard of proof* are to be distinguished according to their different functions.

> —See in general Walker & Walker, The English Legal System, 6th edition, by R.J. Walker, London: Butterworths, 1985, 617, Curzon, Law of Evidence, Plymouth: McDonald & Evans Ltd., 1978, 60, Cross on Evidence (1979), 110, Cross & Wilkins, An Outline of the Law of Evidence (1980), 36, Phipson on Evidence (1982), n. 4-35, Eggleston, Evidence, Proof and Probability (1983), 129, Harry J. Glasbeek, Evidence Cases and Materials, Toronto: Butterworths, 1977, 594

The standard of proof, as we have already seen in our discussion of the evidential burden, is the measure for assessing a certain proof being *adequate and sufficient* for proving a certain fact. Generally put, standard of proof is thus a measure for the adequateness of the proof presented.

All evidence must meet a certain standard to be adequate, to be sufficient; as a result, all evidence has to be evaluated by the judge for meeting the standard of proof applicable in the particular litigation.

This is a very important function of the judge and it's because of this function that the saying is that for a litigation to win, you have to pass the judge; the next step, then, convincing the jury is the final or ultimate burden.

For example, if a good lawyer on the defendant's side, who wants to avoid the unpredictable verdict of a jury, can convince the judge that the evidence presented by the plaintiff is insufficient for meeting the standard of proof, the trial will end here, and it will be ended not by the jury, but by the judge. The verdict will be that the plaintiff was not able to establish a *prima face case* for his allegations.

As a general rule, the standard of proof is a *preponderance of probability.*

> —James & Hazard, Civil Procedure (1977), §7.6, 243: 'The usual formulation of the test in civil cases is that there must be a preponderance of evidence in favour of the party having the persuasion burden (the proponent) before he is entitled to a verdict'. See also Lilly, An Introduction to the Law of Evidence (1978) 41: ' … in a typical civil case, a party must prove the elements of his claim by a preponderance of the evidence (sometimes expressed by the phrases 'greater weight of the evidence' or 'more probable than not'). The same is stated for Canada in the U.L.C.C. Report 1982, §2.3(a), 23.

Cross on Evidence speaks of three standards of proof in the American evidence law; if this standard differs from what is recognized as standard of proof in British law, is however not explicated by the author.

Cross on Evidence

> Three standards of proof appear to be recognized in the United States, proof by 'clear, strong and cogent' evidence laying midway between proof on a preponderance of probability and proof beyond reasonable doubt.

—Cross on Evidence (1979), pp. 111 ff., 118

A fact is proven when the proof submitted by one party has a surplus of probability over the proof submitted by the other party, or, in the words of Lord Denning '… if the evidence is such that the tribunal can say we think it more probable than not'.

—Miller v. Minister of Pensions, [1947] 2 All E R 372, 373-374.

On the other hand, when the probabilities are equal, the fact is not proven.

In case of a *non liquet,* a situation where it's impossible for the judge to make a finding of the fact, it's the persuasion burden that as it were renders the decision: the party that bears the persuasion burden will lose the trial.

Finding of a fact means 'determining that its existence is more probable than its non-existence.'

> —See Model Code on Evidence (1942), Rule 1(5)

Like the evidential burden, the persuasive burden is always related to a particular issue or fact; that is why we have to distinguish the facts that are at the basis of the action, and those at the basis of the defense.

However, this distinction is often simplified when its about the facts that are constituent for the action.

For example, Lord Edmund Davis states in the case *Chapman v. Oakleigh Animal Products, Ltd* that 'the golden rule is that the onus of proof is on the plaintiff'.

—[1970] 8 KIR 1063, 1072

Presumptions are particular in that they link several facts, generally two, as the *Model Code on Evidence (1942)* stipulates in its Rule 701:

> ### Model Code of Evidence
> (1) *Basic Fact*
> Basic fact means the fact or group of facts giving rise to a presumption.
> (2) *Presumption/Presumed Fact*
> Presumption means that when a basic fact exists the existence of another fact must be assumed, whether or not the other fact may be rationally found from the basic fact. Presumed fact means that fact which must be assumed.
>
> —Model Code on Evidence (1942), Rule 701, p. 312

Presumptions influence the burden of proof, however, only the evidential burden; they do not shift the persuasion burden.

> —Walker & Walker, The English Legal System (1985), pp. 606-610, Halsbury's Laws of England, §§111 ff., Cross on Evidence (1979), pp. 121 ff., Phipson on Evidence (1982), n. 4-23 ff., Phipson & Elliott, Manual of the Law of Evidence (1980), p. 75, Lilly, An Introduction to the Law of Evidence (1978), p. 47, Model Code on Evidence (1942), pp. 306 ff.

Rule 301 of the Federal Rules of Evidence, applicable for proceedings in United States federal courts, stipulates this expressly:

> **FEDERAL RULES OF EVIDENCE**
>
> *Rule 301. Presumptions in General in Civil Actions and Proceedings*
> In all civil actions and proceedings not otherwise provided for by Act of Congress or by these rules, a presumption imposes on a party against whom it is directed the burden of going forward with evidence to rebut or meet the presumption, but does not shift to

such party the burden of proof in the sense of the risk of nonpersuasion, which remains throughout the trial upon the party on whom it was originally set.

Notion and Function

The persuasive burden represents, for the party that bears it, the *risk of nonpersuasion*, which is the risk of not being able to convince the trier of fact of a certain alleged issue in trial. It is distinct from the evidential burden in that it never shifts.

> —Wigmore, Evidence in Trials at Common Law (1981), Vol. 9, §2485, Cross & Wilkins, An Outline of the Law of Evidence (1980), 27, Lilly, An Introduction to the Law of Evidence (1978), 41. The term 'trier of fact' is defined in the Model Code on Evidence (1942), Rule 1(14), 72: 'Trier of fact includes a jury, and a judge when is is trying an issue of fact other than one relating to the admissibility of evidence.'

This is why the persuasive burden is also called fixed burden of proof.

> —See, for example, Glasbeek, Evidence Cases and Materials (1977), 634, Halsbury's Laws of England, §13, Phipson on Evidence (1982), 47 n. 4-07, Lilly, An Introduction to the Law of Evidence (1978), 45, Graham, Federal Rules in a Nutshell (1981), §301.5, 45

It always stays with the party that bears it due to the applicable substantive law or the pleadings.

> —Cross on Evidence (1979), 87. Halsbury's Laws of England, §13, Phipson on Evidence (1982), n. 4-06. Sometimes, in the literature there is question of a 'burden of pleadings'. The expression however is awkward as the burden of pleadings can't be a valid guideline for finding out about the incidence of the persuasive burden.

For this reason, it also is called *ultimate burden*, while we have seen that the evidential burden is a provisional burden. The reason why this burden does not shift is its *procedural function*; it is not related to the production of evidence but enters the stage after all evidence has been produced: it then allows to render a verdict in favor of one party.

Cross & Wilkins

> The burden of proof is crucial when all evidence is in. It makes itself felt at a later stage than the burden of adducing evidence.

—Cross & Wilkins, An Outline of the Law of Evidence (1980), 27. See also Curzon, Law of Evidence (1978), §5, 48, Phipson and Elliott, Manual of the Law of Evidence (1980), 51, Lilly, An Introduction to the Law of Evidence (1978), 41

Incidence

The general rule is *ei qui affirmat non ei qui negat incumbit probatio*.

That means the one who affirms a fact, be it positive or negative, must prove it, and not the one who contests the fact. In this simple rule, there are contained actually three different principles:

- (1) The one who affirms a fact must prove it;
- (2) The one who contests a fact is not obliged to prove his negation of the fact;
- (3) The one who affirmatively contests a fact must prove his affirmative defense.

> —Phipson on Evidence (1982), n. 4-02, Eggleston, Evidence, Proof and Probability (1983), 103. A synonymous expression is 'ei incumbit probatio qui dicit, non qui negat', see Cross on Evidence (1979)

Only facts that are contested need to be proven. This is a general principle valid for all jurisdictions.

It is both logical and reasonable to put the burden of proof on the party that invokes a right as a lawful consequence of certain alleged facts.

This is in the general case the plaintiff or the party that would lose the trial if there was no evidence in court.

> —Glasbeek, Evidence Cases and Materials (1977), 634: 'Each party will wish to have certain facts found so that the pertinent substantive law will be applied in his favour. Accordingly, it is logical to place the risk of non-persuasion, i.e. the legal burden, in respect of each fact-in-issue on the party who will fail in his claim if the fact-in-issue is not found to exist.' See Cross & Wilkins, An Outline of the Law of Evidence (1980), 28: 'The question is usually not a particularly difficult one, for a fundamental requirement of any judicial system is that the person who desires the court to take action must prove his case to its satisfaction. This means that, as a matter of common sense, the burden of proving of all facts to their claim normally rests upon the plaintiff.' See also Cross on Evidence (1979), 96 and Halsbury's Laws of England, §14: 'The legal burden of proof normally rests upon the party desiring the court to take action; thus a claimant must satisfy the court or tribunal that the conditions which entitle him to an award have been satisfied,'

> citing Dickinson v. Minister of Pensions, [1953] 1 Q.B. 228, 232, [1952] 2 All E R 1031, 1033.

The burden of proof for the affirmation of a fact also encompasses the burden of proof for the negation of a fact, also called *burden of disproof*, if the party who bears the burden of proof alleges the nonexistence of a fact, or its negation.

This is to say that the burden of proof is something functional in a trial, and not dependent on the nature of the allegations.

> —Cross and Wilkins, An Outline of the Law of Evidence (1980), 28: 'The rule is sometimes expressed in such maxims as 'he who affirms must prove', but this must not be taken to mean that the burden of proof cannot lie upon a party who makes a negative allegation. There are numerous instances in which the plaintiff or prosecutor assumes the burden of proving a negative. (...) In these cases the phrase 'burden of proof' includes the burden of disproof'. See also Wigmore, Evidence in Trials at Common

> Law (1981), Vol. 9, §2484, 288: 'The burden is often on one who has a negative assertion to prove.'

In principle, in all cases except affirmative defenses, the burden of proof is on the plaintiff. In addition, it has to be noted that the burden of proof is on the party who adds a new element to the pleadings.

> —Graham, Federal Rules of Evidence in a Nutshell (1981), §301.2, 41 and Carlson v. Nelson, 285 N.W.2d 505, 204 Neb.765 (Neb.1979)

To recapitulate, the evidential burden follows the legal burden.

Even as far as affirmative defenses are concerned, the evidential burden follows the legal burden: in that situation both burdens are on the defendant for establishing the affirmative defense.

THE BURDEN OF PROOF

—Coast Pump Associates v. Stephen Tyler Corp., 133 Cal.Rptr.88, 62 C.A.3d (Cal.App.1976) and Booth Newspapers Inc., v. Regents of University of Michigan, 280 N.W.2d 883, 90 Mich.App.99 (Mich.App. 1979).

BIBLIOGRAPHY

Contextual Bibliography

ADEDE, A.D.

The United Kingdom Abandons the Doctrine of Absolute Sovereign Immunity
6 BROOKLYN J. INT'L L. 1997-215 (1980)

AGUDA, AKINOLA

Law and Practice Relating to Evidence in Nigeria
LONDON: SWEET & MAXWELL, 1980

AMERICAN LAW INSTITUTE

Model Code on Evidence
CHESTNUT, PHILADELPHIA, 1942

AUSTRALIA

The Law Reform Commission
REFORM OF EVIDENCE LAW 1980
DISCUSSION PAPER N° 16
CANBERRA: AUSTRALIAN GOVERNMENT PUBLISHING SERVICE, 1980

Bennion, Francis

Statutory Interpretation
London: Butterworths, 1984

Cairns, Bernard C.

Australian Civil Procedure
Sydney: The Law Book Company Ltd., 1981

Canada

Uniform Evidence Act, Livre II
Règles Générales de Preuve, Titre I, Fardeau de la Preuve

Report of the Federal/Provincial Task Force on Uniform Rules of Evidence
Prepared for the Uniform Law Conference of Canada
Toronto: The Carswell Company Ltd., 1982 [U.L.C.C. Report]

Coyne, Thomas A.

Rules of Civil Procedure for the United States District Courts
Practice Comments
New York: Clark Boardman Company Ltd., 1983

BIBLIOGRAPHY

CROSS, SIR RUPERT

Cross on Evidence
5TH ED.
LONDON: BUTTERWORTHS, 1979

Cross on Evidence
2ND AUSTRALIAN EDITION
BY J.A. GOBBO, DAVID BYRNE, J.D. HEYDON
SIDNEY: BUTTERWORTHS, 1980

CROSS, SIR RUPERT & WILKINS, NANCY

An Outline of the Law of Evidence
5TH EDITION
LONDON: BUTTERWORTHS, 1980

CURZON, L.B.

Law of Evidence
PLYMOUTH: MCDONALD & EVANS LTD., 1978

EGGLESTON, SIR RICHARD

Evidence, Proof and Probability
2ND EDITION
LONDON: WEIDENFELS & NICHOLSON, 1983

Glasbeek, Harry J.

Evidence Cases and Materials
Toronto: Butterworths, 1977

Cases and Materials on Evidence
Australian Edition
Sydney: Butterworths, 1974

Graham, Michael H.

Evidence
Text, Rules, Illustrations and Problems
The Commentary Method
St. Paul (Minn.): National Institute for Trial Advocacy, 1983

Federal Rules of Evidence in a Nutshell
St. Paul (Minn.): American Textbook Series, 1981

Harvard University

A Uniform System of Citation
13th Edition
Cambridge, Mass.: Harvard Law Review Association, 1982

BIBLIOGRAPHY

Hoffmann & Zeffert

South African Law of Evidence
3RD EDITION
DURBAN: BUTTERWORTHS, 1983

James, Fleming & Hazard, Geoffrey

Civil Procedure
2ND EDITION

Jowitt's Dictionary of English Law

2nd Edition, by John Burke
LONDON: SWEET & MAXWELL, 1977

Lal, Jadgish

Code of Civil Procedure, 1908
AS AMENDED UP TO DATE BY C.P.C. AMENDMENT ACT N° 104 OF 1976
ALLAHABAD: LAW PUBLISHERS SARDAR PATEL, 1981

Lilly, Graham C.

An Introduction to the Law of Evidence
ST. PAUL (WEST), 1978

Maxwell on the Interpretation of Statutes

12th ed., by P. St. J. Langan
London: Sweet & Maxwell, 1969

McCormick

McCormick on Evidence
by Edward W. Cleary, 3d ed.
Lawyers Edition (Homebook Series)
St. Paul: West, 1984

Moore, James W.

Moore's Federal Practice
2nd Edition, 1979

Nash, Gerard

Civil Procedure
Cases and Text
Sydney: The Law Book Company Ltd., 1976

Ninth Decennial Digest

American Digest System
Part I, 1976-1981

Phipson

Phipson on Evidence
13TH ED., BY JOHN HUXLEY BUZZARD
RICHARD MAY AND M. N. HOWARD
LONDON: SWEET & MAXWELL, 1982

Phipson and Elliott

Manual of the Law of Evidence
11TH EDITION
BY D. W. ELLIOTT
LONDON: SWEET & MAXWELL, 1980

Rothstein, Paul F.

Evidence in a Nutshell: State and Federal Rules
2ND EDITION
ST. PAUL (WEST), 1981

Row, Sanjiva

Code of Civil Procedure (Act V of 1908)
BY MALIK
3RD EDITION, VOL. 1
ALLAHABAD: LAW BOOK COMPANY, 1962

Rules of Civil Procedure for the United States District Courts

Practice Comments by Thomas A. Coyne
New York: Clark Boardman Company Ltd., 1983

Sarkar's Law of Evidence

India, Pakistan, Bangladesh, Burma & Ceylon
13th Edition
by Prabhas C. Sarkar and Sudipto Sarkar
Calcutta: S. C. Sarkar & Sons, 1981

Sarkar on Civil Procedure

6th Edition, as amended by Act 104 of 1976
by Prabhas C. Sarkar and Sudipto Sarkar
Calcutta: S. C. Sarkar & Sons, 1979

Smith, P. F. / Bailey, S.

The Modern English Legal System
London: Sweet & Maxwell, 1984

Sutherland

Statutory Construction
Ed. By Sands
4th Edition
London, 1975

Tayer, James Bradley

A Preliminary Treatise on Evidence
1898

The English and Empire Digest

Vol. 22, 'Evidence'
London: Butterworths, 1974

Walker & Walker

The English Legal System
6th Edition, by R.J. Walker
London: Butterworths, 1985

WIGMORE, JOHN HENRY

A Treatise on the Anglo-American System of Evidence in Trials at Common Law
10 VOLUMES, VOL. 9 'EVIDENCE IN TRIALS AT COMMON LAW'
REV. BY JAMES H. CHADBURN
BOSTON, TORONTO: LITTLE, BROWN & COMPANY, 1981

WOODROFFE & AMER ALI

Law of Evidence
14TH EDITION
ED. AND REV. BY B. R. P. SINGHAL AND NARAYAN DAS
ALLAHABAD: LAW BOOK COMPANY LTD., 1979

WORDS AND PHRASES LEGALLY DEFINED

Ed. by John B. Saunders
2ND EDITION
LONDON: BUTTERWORTHS, 1969

WRIGHT, MILLER & COOPER

Federal Practice and Procedure, 1975

Personal Notes

Personal Notes

Personal Notes

Personal Notes

Personal Notes

www.ingramcontent.com/pod-product-compliance
Lightning Source LLC
Chambersburg PA
CBHW021019180526
45163CB00005B/2025